YOUR
ENZYMES
ARE
CALLING
THE
ANCIENTS

ALSO BY
KAREN DONOVAN

Fugitive Red

Your Enzymes Are Calling the Ancients

Poems

Karen Donovan

WINNER OF THE 2015
LEXI RUDNITSKY
EDITOR'S CHOICE AWARD

A Karen & Michael Braziller Book
PERSEA BOOKS
New York

Persea Books, Inc.
277 Broadway
New York, NY 10007

Library of Congress Cataloging-in-Publication Data

Names: Donovan, Karen, 1956– author.
Title: Your enzymes are calling the ancients : poems / Karen Donovan.
Description: New York : A Karen & Michael Braziller Book/Persea Books, [2016=]
Identifiers: LCCN 2016022139 | ISBN 9780892554768 (softcover : acid-free paper)
Classification: LCC PS3554.O554 A6 2016 | DDC 811/.54—dc23
LC record available at https://lccn.loc.gov/2016022139

First edition
Printed in the United States of America
Designed by Rita Lascaro

FOR WALKER

Contents

YOUR
ENZYMES
ARE
CALLING
THE
ANCIENTS

Parts List Counted in Ogham

: the alphabetic system of 5th and 6th century Old Irish in which an alphabet of 20 letters is represented by notches for vowels and lines for consonants and which is known principally from inscriptions cut on the edges of rough standing tombstones

⊢

: a tufted marsh plant

But I am already attached:
you, me, the nutsedge.

The way it unfolded from black loam
and July rain and spread sweetly once I cleared
rank jimson and panic grass.
Green blade, tell me, am I not to attach?
Oh, I am most pagan with respect to trees!
My confession: I have also refused to pull up
the velvet leaf and a twining pea.

Into haunted solitude: the weedpile
turning to straw, the yellow moon.

⊨

: an envelope of rays emanating from a point and reflected or refracted
by a curved surface

What I most love: the bright caustic,
rippled light on the ceiling as sun
breaking the treeline bounces off water,
incidental spectra painted on a wall
·or, there, that nimbus thrown from the lip
of your tumbler.

You do not know how to point to or define the meaning,
you lack any formula or image for it,
and yet it is more certain for you than the sensations of your senses

The nearly concealed dimensions of the everywhere.

E

: an arboreal chiefly nocturnal mammal

And let us decide right now about the lemur.
Do we not love the lemur with our whole hearts and our whole minds?
Do we not also wish to return home soon to Madagascar,
where we will all speak the balanced, balletic language of the body?
What is the meaning of a bubble from the bottom of the sea?
the mythologist of the psyche asks.

You must convince the lemur to give you the ring
from his storied tail.

E

: an insect that feeds on other insects and clasps its prey in forelimbs
held up as if in prayer

Regarding the mantis, let us at least be truthful
about the thrill of witnessing
the voracious grasshopper reverently dispatched
by a creature so suited to the task.
We are grateful
        at a distance.
We are regretful
        at a distance.
About the temptation to imagine ourselves at a distance.

It is impossible to prefigure the salvation of the world
in the same language
by which the world has been dismembered and defaced
As if the possibility of the act
of thanksgiving were sufficient to conclude
anything at all.

: an opaque cryptocrystalline quartz

Mud, under pressure, crushes to sunset
multilayer cake, moss-black, sienna, ochre, dark red,
splinters in slow-mo like brown bones
as the earth rolls its insides up.

This is how the jasper comes to me,
gravel in a plain Iowa riverbed,
ghost boats drifting downstream,
fishlines out, motor cut,

how you come to me
in a gesture common as sand,
the commonest gesture of the open hand,
warm wind in leaves, deep sigh
of someone sleeping.
Why may they not be the actual
turning-places and growing-places which they seem to be,
of the world—why not the workshop of being

As this fractured pebble, me,
final indivisible thing here, yours.

⊣

: any of various small fish that are less than a designated size and are not game fish

Though they are
the calculus: minnow
then minnow then
minnow then minnow.
We are not persuaders
We are the children of the Unknown,

discrete linearity innumerably agreeing into

curves that stream through the eelgrass
on brackish late summer tides
and demonstrate closer to home
how the great mathematicians
solved the planetary orbits
by computing in fish flicks.

⊐

: fuzz especially consisting of fine ravelings

And fast by hanging in a golden chain
This pendant world

Contrast: pocket lint.
Further reading: ontological shock vs. the circus catch.

The lack of consolation.
Whether postmodern materialism constitutes a second fall.

Exhibit notes: cyclades figures, votive statues, eye idols.
Dilmun the original paradise.

: radiation situated beyond the visible spectrum at its violet end

Past the reef-edge where color sifts out from all containers,
the abyssal, other side of depth, what the very ancients called
abzu, primeval waters,
sojourners to that ultraviolet would obtain
their tickets with proviso: You will not come back.
Thus I am now returned in Spirit as a Heavenly Spy
because I could not explain why
I knew there was someplace else to go,
someplace better,

because no stop sign is fail-safe.

: a piece of mail that is undeliverable because [it is] illegibly or incorrectly addressed

Virginia,
Heard today this definition of "nixie" will be deleted from all new editions of Merriam-Webster's Collegiate; thought you'd want to know. Went straightaway to my bookshelf to check, language being, as so much else in our overly policed age, basically use it or lose it. There it sits on page 800, a bit below "nitwit," still wheezing like a little appendix, unaware of the looming editorial scalpel that will excise it from the body textual. For now, they are leaving in the first definition, which you will appreciate. *It would seem to be something very erratic, very undependable— now to be found in a dusty road, now in a scrap of newspaper in the street, now in a daffodil in the sun.* This leafboat my messenger.
Regards,

: a mythical animal having the power to endure fire without harm

O salamander, my shepherd,
is it true? *The disciple simply burns his boats and goes ahead*

The drunken alchemist claimed you
became the flame and so were not consumed
but revealed most perfectly to being
of the same substance fundamental of the cosmos,
dark edge of dark ponds, that substance
we last breathed through lost gills, far from home.

Old soul, I followed you
out of one cosmos and into another, discovering
how the body can be unmade
and remade also by maple light
and green rain falling steadily onto the earth.

+

: a procedure for solving a mathematical problem in a finite number of steps that frequently involves repetition of an operation

cirrus stratus cirrostratus
      jack pine
      tamarack
      spruce
altostratus cumulonimbus
      jack pine
      tamarack
      spruce
split pea split second
archangelic algorithm
Invisible wings are given to us too
tawee tawee tawee-tee-to
chick-a-dee-dee-dee
toooo tititi twee tititi tititi tititi
toooo tititi twee tititi tititi tititi
wicka wicka wicka wicka
chick-a-dee-dee-dee
chick-a-dee-dee-dee
spirogyra equinox
licorice dickcissel
      jack pine
      tamarack
      spruce

‡

: any of family Ixodidae whose young cling to bushes whence they
readily drop on and attach themselves to passing animals where
they may produce troublesome sores or serve as vectors for disease-
producing microorganisms

Want the wood but not the wood tick?
Try ChemLawn.
Toxic to high-quality targets: weeds grassy and broadleaf,
sucker bugs that wreck the roses,
fish, bees, birds, the neighbor's pets, anyone's kids,
including your own. Got grubs?
Wild violet or nimblewill?
They're out there in the dark. Listen:
All those things men tell of down in hell,
far under the earth, are right here in our lives

‡

: the star of the northern hemisphere toward which the axis of the earth
points

The sense of a construction more enduring than the self.
No less of a construction but the chiefest
of made things. The sense of a floor.

A conviction the landscape carries,
for instance, masterfully turning us
under Polaris no matter which door you step from.

The ethic emerging in the struggle
has as its main theme not prudence but existential courage

A construction, if it were possible, a sense
of the floor, an allegiance
to it, and if it were possible then, liberty.

```
 ┿
═╪═
═╪═
 ┿
```

: a dense variously colored and usually lustrous concretion

First the error,
then the bludgeoning,
then the pearl.
First the imagining,
then the pavement,
then the language.

New tortures have been invented
for the madmen who have brought good news

The above, the below,
the dividing line.

‡

: a hill or ridge of sand piled up by the wind

April. Cold dune.
Soon the clouds gathered and opened
to show what was gathered beyond.
A dog barked from a lawn
down the beach. A gull mewled.
I do believe that you can deepen
your own orthodoxy
if you are not afraid of strange visions
When I made a request,
it was not: lead my army.

Reversing the way back
through the park, I leaned to study
catkins strewn over the path,
then the door to the port-a-john slammed
and sparrows chorused rose briars, my license
to love the world finally
as much as I could or be damned.

＋

: moisture condensed upon the surfaces of cool bodies especially at night

They also say of dew: It falls.
As though from the sky, iridescent on the grass
at dawn in haloes around the bent places
where we slept together,
out under stars that pierced us with old light,

it fell like dew
on the rocks and the blossoms,
on us, till we woke soaking wet,
no longer dreaming, and shivering
embraced as if for the first time.

And then we who are not all wise think
that everything which we have undertaken
was all nothing

Looking back at myself in your eyes
I could see it had fallen on us
like knowledge, that food we would need
to learn how to eat on the way, the long walk
it would be.

ǂ

: an inscription or drawing made on some public surface

Graffiti as tattoo, as surgical scar.
The symbol squats on a fact.

Are you living or just buying?

A labyrinth has no dead ends.
          [Now you tell me.]

You might consider your pain as a focusing tool.
          [I might consider YOUR pain as a focusing tool.]

A rhetoric as a collection, a thicket of skipperlings.
He left an ichthys in the urinal.

♯

: a venomous or reputedly venomous snake

So if the future is a viper
coiled at the bottom of an onyx jar
and in we must reach, why imagine
another future? *Every angel is terrifying*

Or if the bronzed ribbon tangled
in lavender this morning flicks its forked
tongue, look at us, already flooded
with namelessness.

‡

: a low heavy continuous reverberating often muffled sound

in this stillness   the light blinds
what we imagine is coming
what the silence means   what the stillness
of what is coming
this   rumble
tumbling the darkness of it
listen for it listen

stillness the dark   the blind will
but what silence means   what the
surroundings will say in this stillness
of what awaiting
O   listen
is just the unspeakable
silence of the silence

: a very small pool
: a bed or receptacle prepared by a bird

: any of a family of colonial hymenopterous insects with a complex social
organization and various castes performing special duties

: an open bowl-shaped drinking vessel
: an injury to the body that involves laceration or breaking of a membrane

: an unstressed mid-central vowel
: the seedy edible fruit of various brambles

puddle | nest | ant | cup | wound | schwa | blackberry . . .

There was only one thing to be done: call out,
start the alarm, set the heather on fire

Questions of Scale

We dip our paddles in the brown Chippewa
      and pull upstream under a broad porch of beech.

Can't do this at home, I joke, imagining any
      of Alabama's famous snakes clanging into the canoe,

hello! Like that guy who blew the head off a cottonmouth
      dropped in his boat so fast he forgot himself,

    got the stern, sank it straight.
Peeps panic at the water edge.

✕ ✕ ✕

    Round the first bend your voice spills
past me in tributaries, *blue heron to port.*

    Taking note, he lifts his greatcoat
and floats a singlet flap,

    sticklike legs retracting past the S-curve.
Hornets' nest hangs, paper planet,

    beyond, triad of inscrutable waxwings.
No wind, whorls coming off my strokes,

a presence perhaps steering:
eloquent silence shaped as heron.

✕ ✕ ✕

Once I walked through the house praising
  the day's solidity. Ox-eye daisy, bunchberry,

dragon's mouth, galaxy of wild carrot
  draped by pale slips, summer bluets flying coupled,

is and isn't. Decay of the false vacuum
  physicists call the expansion of the universe,

as if true vacuum doesn't explain enough,
  but no there's always before before

whence all the debaters jump to their feet in disgust.
  The one who remains confronts the assembly,

deserted grandstand littered with tickets,
  and starts to speak.

✕ ✕ ✕

  Why I wanted to lay down more weight,
little ruby pawprint garlands through the rooms,

  that ventilation hood in which spun whirlpools
of amber liquid sustained by rotating magnets,

  such was chemistry. A charred mitt hung on a peg,
tubing and glass clamped a trellis,

  the creator had left her safety goggles
hooked on the last rung.

xxx

Why I wanted a blue more insistent
to record the number of steps I could take

before I forgot my name.
Why we were always arriving, adding zeroes

up or down the architecture
nested infinite wherever we deplaned,

landscape stamped halfway between us and out there
like a drive-in movie screen rising from the marsh

in a veil of mosquitoes. The heroine's
final scene stands against a backdrop of stars

as a fixed measure of longing.
Why we were the only ones weeping.

xxx

I rest the paddle across my knees
and lean forward. The river unspools

from upended oaks,
there, yellow eye level as horizon.

The canoe resolves
to rolled-up mental space of heron-event

some growable indiscriminate
ratio of layer cake

while the current floats us back.
Why it holds, why it never ends.

✕ ✕ ✕

Later, even at the end above the trees in Boötes
tonight, the bear guard Arcturus fires orange-red,

and at a lighted window a man
is plucking each string and singing,

I know where I'm going, and I know
who's going with me,

I know who I love,
but the dear knows who I'll marry.

Extracurricular

i. Identify

False duality / dichotomy

      Identify the excluded middle
The not male not female

Identify the categories as categories
      The logic which is helpful but does not inhere

Under soldiers roses Under roses ships Under ships ballerinas Under ballerinas hens and chicks Under hens and chicks mountain streams Under mountain streams books Under books more books Under more books angelfish Under angelfish planets Under planets pansies Under pansies kitchenware Under kitchenware city scenes Under city scenes stripes Under stripes plaids Under plaids etc.

      Under the onion the notonion

ii. Describe

The scribe / de-scribing
herself: a tendency

to leave her clothes around
in disrobe order / socks on top

Peel up / stick down
Watch out: flamethrower

iii. Compare

Clarify the basis for comparison pleeze
Is there an annual fee?

Or forget the basis for comparison:

> a. Woman at TCBY with entire prosthetic eye socket
> b. "Sweet energetic little multifloral dwarf"
> c. Caryatid
> d. Shamanic body mutilation—nightmare???
> e. Fire ants
> f. All is linked (Leibniz)

You bee the glue

iv. Explain

Thus / begins / thermodynamics

Stacked / restacked

Body in the street
Body in the doorway
Body falling
Face crumpling
Arms going up

> This film does not run backwards

Body in the woods
Body in the cell
Body falling
Mouth opening
Eyes opening

This film does not run backwards

v. Interpret

All eggs stand for eggs
For "sand" read "the firmament"
When I say "I," have in mind the provisional I

For surface the operation is: scratch
For depth: plumb

The Plumose

"This is this" (she said)

vi. Speculate

Uhhhh ... yaaa ... whoa ... eeek

(thumbprint of diminishing functions)

vii. Analyze

Identify the categories / as categories

Very useful shoeboxes / yet shoeboxes nonetheless

Perhaps a hammer / perhaps not

Or redraw everything:

A firetruck	hammer
A lily	hammer
A bedspread	hammer
A hammered	hammer

Now just
Now just

viii. Conclude

    The world is not new
When I say "we," I mean we

as a multiplicity, a unity, what it was
    Wild mint, the ground where it grew

Nine Pictographs and a
Slight Correlation to a Lyric by Elvis

They catch too many so the kids pitch fish

at each other in hysterics then bait
the wire trap with the last of the breadballs.

Ah,
little fins, you go for it, always
it's your dumb, blameless hunger. It's a fact

children want to learn how to play: minnows
swim into traps. The rest is extra,

bodies impaled on sticks, lost in tangled

grass grown cold with nightfall. They get called in
for dinner. Perishing blossom, listen,

he sang, *tear it all apart, but love me.*

         ✘ ✘ ✘

And that red bird my heart. Pyrotechnic
irises shooting off Roman candles

from the seawall, lagoon swollen with tide,
all buds burst, a whorled seductive surface

I want appears. Here what mystery this

itchy libidinous joy radiates,
here drink it, the great fountain of eros,

the boundary crosser, the cross-dresser,

category dissolver, best solvent
for hesitancy, temptation's trumpet

flower in the surge, ka-thump ka-thump ka-

thump, everything I say I want, every
one. Heat and light beat a seesaw rhythm

difficult to interpret mid-sentence,

a body makes its declarations, pulls
to orbit irresistibly ideas

and other minds, strict attractive fluid

force of creation itself looking for
release, for reasons we were made this way.

⚔ ⚔ ⚔

Sanctus spiritus.
                In an old
                photo,

I'm squinting bucktoothed at the camera,
standing in the lot at Saint Margaret's,

still tonguing the nontaste of the wafer.
It's like eating paper but easier,
I later tell my little brother who

isn't listening. When the church burns down
I am grown and long gone out of that town.

I can fit my thumb over the image
of me in a white dress, white crown and veil
(here's grandmother Nellie in her big hat,

my father smiling, a Kodak blue sky),
but underneath my thumb, I am still there,

a look like worry on my face as if
I could foresee the wandering ahead.

Everyone else
        in the picture
        is dead.

x x x

        It was said the man
        mixed clay with
        his spit

as a poultice for blindness. It was said
the prophet's tongue received a burning coal

        and yet burned
        thereupon
        only with words.

If I am conjuring, let innocence
answer. It was said that one touch can wake

the dead
weight of the mind
and carry it

home on the stem of a lily. If I
am conjuring, let innocence answer.

✕ ✕ ✕

A sand dollar broken into quarters.
An osprey climbing out of a spiral.

Signify: the axle assembly was
slinging lubricant from the pinion seal.

Somewhere I read about the caddisworm,
the larva of a caddisfly, whose home
is a silken case stuck outside with trash,

old dead leaves and sticks it drags around, fat
on algae at the bottom of some pond,
camouflaged until its wings are finished.

A very cute trick, although the journey
to that far surface is nowhere described.

Quahoggers off Nayatt Point fade to gray
across the leaden silver wave moiré.

✕ ✕ ✕

Refusal to acknowledge beauty is
a failure of nerve, so acknowledge it:

screen door slams, summer evening, my neighbor
fends off mosquitoes, standing and calling

the names of his children, and every night
always the one who will never reply,

every time, who he must go out and find.
Three bells chime, bells are twining each leaf on

the vine, spreading wide its branching green palm
as he passes the last golden chime down the
                                        line
                        down the line
                down the line
                        line
                        line
                                        line

                ✘ ✘ ✘

        Test the spirits.
We have so mistaken

flame in the shape of the body
        for lust,

any moment of speech
        for possession,

have measured dimensions of the planet
using infinitely malleable

        shadows, ours,
as a standard unit. Here

        they are as fists, here attenuated
as bridges, late afternoon stilting through

the dry meadow across the road.
                    When I

turn to you your eyes blaze up like watered

          sunlight. We have been taught
only some things.

                         ✕ ✕ ✕

          To tell
so color can approximate

          the sky
                    blue inside the curved line moving
about and below the close horizon,

          the chord
ringing in the spine, pale grass, all

          ideas
                    of order. I am pointing, now
follow my hand outline snowy hillsides

          or section
an orange, still it's only

          pointing:
                    a white bowl, a flame, three herons
fishing. If one were to say the self is

          a bowl,
fills water and brims over, wells

and spills
        abundance to be this singing.
Oh that yes I had a thousand voices.

              ⅗ ⅗ ⅗

Talk radio strays from rusty pickups.

The whole morning long a fisherman spreads
        his feet on broken oystershells, casting

casting, the thin screeee of the line peeling
        off a reel, mixed with cries of early gulls

scheming each other over stolen food,
        pitiless in pursuit of a prize dropped

plop on the tideline, some cracked, wretched crab
        still waving its one good leg. His line casts

and gulls wheel past the first channel buoy
        and water erupts with baitfish leaping

from darkness where cooler swifter water
        streams in from the bay. We all of us shout

and point: mayhem on the surface signals
        something huge and deep, in an instant flick

the house catches fire, fish slapping at
        exits getting nowhere fast and he goes

there knowing, *big ones below.* He goes there.

✕ ✕ ✕

Testimony Concerning Diatoms

How talk tends to stop when anyone asks
        do you know what a throwoff lever is

How everything plus everything equals
How a geometer might attempt to
prove the principle of fecundity

to a physicist with glue on his hands
        How it would be good to know more about

everything especially chloroplasts
How I still have to sneak up on meaning
by peeling off its adhesive backing

How *primum* quite *mobile* their tiny
        but voluminous moods tending toward bloom

How during our conversation last week
she wept so when I mentioned her mother
How I had to research the difference

then between who I was and why I was
        How that line Whalen wrote sticks to my coat

How he was *conscious even while sleeping*
How if the kingdom that has already
broken into this world has not yet come

×××

How a rain rose and fell and rose again
      How two sparrows in a mossy tree spoke

with each other until others arrived
How the neighbor's dog barked to be let in
How our weapons came already sharpened

How they had their hands all on my daylight
      How after thought so How written down wrong

How someone in the hallway is playing
with the dimmer switch and why they won't stop
How my transparent cilia got me

out of more than one jam let me tell you
      How rage + entropy balanced a stone

How the archive brimmed with porphyrin rings
How items were graphed that were graphable
How you can be blessed and still get eaten

How an answer could be: hydrozoan
      How a lost child invokes many mothers

How lament is sure to cook a clambake
How I desired a torch and you gave me
a candle saying this is all you need

×××

How five sand crabs in a bucket are worth
      more than a price you pay for a bucket

How what I forgot returned with a sting
sharper than my original error
How composition has an accident

with the gods of disorder with themselves
            hoping meanwhile nobody is watching

How photophosphorylation it is
How the centerline got even greener
How oh How let me get my camera out

How I lost that electron you gave me
            and then married the invisible world

How *a ghost dancer walks in a black hat*
through gates of horn may well be my memoir
How I can thank the poet monk for that

How I disobeyed until my last breath
            and then decided to do all you asked

How perch fly in the talons of ospreys
stunned by perspectives indelibly far
above these onrushing waves in the trees

                        ✗ ✗ ✗

How landscape scrolled up like a window shade
            How too much of one thing and not ever

of another tripped the precinct alarm
How a shoeshine talked me off my trapeze
How when you wanted me to use the word

contingency in a sentence I did
            How [foghorn screech owl cricket] orchestrates

a soundtrack beneath my insomnia
How I sat in the dark sanctuary
drinking a chocolate milkshake and thinking

How the trail dappled and a stream ran through
How that seagull feather sailed a dozen

spirals floating downward to the sidewalk
while the next bus waited to take a left
How that still won't keep my heart from breaking

How I attempted to boil the ocean
with a preponderance of soothsaying

How heaven also burns everything up
How the sheet music did arrive on time
How I went with it and you showed me why

x x x

How dragonflies never need furniture
How untangling becomes a real science

How a dog pressed a path in wet cement
and wise ones decided to leave it there
How dessert is often unrecognized

How snails anchor all interpretation
How we could pause time by pinning rivers

with rocks and tornadoes with citations
How thunder charged a footnote to lightning
How water hands us oxygen by means

of a leaf preoccupied with complex
machinery for doing something else

How you fixed your eyes always on ogres
How asphalt turns up with a lobbyist
How it looks less like a plan and more like

hope risking volunteers for ridicule
　　　　How I still can't ping the default gateway

How I can always make something from this
How hummingbirds practice precalculus
and muskrats swim towing wide vees of sky

✕ ✕ ✕

How when I saw you standing in the road
　　　　our brains in phase emitted two photons

How thickness of layer and multiverse
of voice reveal a path for wanderers
How I never knew her last call to me

was her last call to me and how we left
　　　　it at goodnight instead of at goodbye

How if draft mode is what everyone is
aiming to escape then can you explain
the moon erasing its steps every month

How living in this age might compare to
　　　　intricate mistranslations of ourselves

into vedic sanskrit esperanto
How worry is done and money is hay
How irony is never visible

and never clawless in the face of love
　　　　How goblins can still reach their hands into

my shirt and scare me into agreement
How reality like the thermocline
is subject to invasion from elsewhere

✕ ✕ ✕

How alleluia How goldfinch How grass
        How there was disagreement regardless

How her laugh was a house wren spilling out
from a room where some sheet rockers had worked
How a shout lodged between my shoulder blades

How a small white boat nudged off a sandbar
        How as if lit from within the fog shone

How we expertly eluded ladders
that would have welcomed us down from this height
How our progress answered sidewindingly

How the fishermen's voices bounced across
        the cove from the dock ramp at 4 a.m.

waking me then to perfect happiness
How its layering wedges in meaning
How a piano had it memorized

How a millipede ran over the floor
        this morning and I caught it in a cup

How invisibly the callixylon
tree drapes its ancient ferns above our heads
How much magic at base camp there might be

Lost Gospel of Ribosome

In those days we were subject to a certain force of momentum. It prevented us from understanding that the world had ceased to revolve. Soon even the moon was self-adhesive.

Rain today rain tomorrow. We clipped tags on their ears so we could tell the sheep apart.

Horse chestnuts are not like buckeyes at all.

She picked up the very purple stones. I was the one who had forgotten to bring my hands along. He had the power to read people's thoughts, but only on the uptown bus.

Do you recall her face? A photographer was standing in the aisle.

The man cradled his bundle as if it were a sack of bones, which it was.

Her essay discussed the usefulness of "satan" as a heuristic. He said "the cha-cha of grace" and I wrote it down. Perhaps Western thinkers have insufficiently explored the concept of the avatar.

But I thought you liked a nice gladiola. Go on, he couldn't hit a bull in the ass with a banjo.

Can't I just close my eyes for a minute?

The ayatollahs came early and left late. They were too young to be mothers and looked like they needed mothers themselves. In biology we often say, "The cell does this, the cell does that."

It isn't what you say, it's how you say it. She got a piece of that timeshare on Jupiter.

What are you talking about, nothing is like the shape of Argentina.

✗ ✗ ✗

Iris absence / iris violence. The theologian explained that revelation is not universally accepted. Then we got actually scared.

Blue bone / marble petal. Cracked / under the crust.

As I'm trying two words: the earth.

He poured himself another single-remedy scotch. She admitted things. I wanted to see where the cormorant would surface.

Crab carapace / seven swans stamping. When the work was sweet.

A midge hatched right off my spoon.

There's a drug for that. I felt under the cushions for my equations. If she had meant to hurt you she would have tried even harder.

What's the watchword? We have ossified, he was sure of it.

They're doing the Caesar salad.

Rotund / humdinger. Brocade / beef waffles. The logos beetled up and wandered off the page.

They agreed that reality lately had a stun-gun aspect. How can you just stand there?

I came here for the waters.

✕ ✕ ✕

He sang the news and was shouted down. For God's sake, Irene. But everything *is* a test!

What is the strategy? What are the tactics? *[cartoon sound effects]*

You might consider this an S-O-S.

The postman spoke in phonemes. Includes, contains, is composed of. Pour me some of that.

He reminded the stockholders that "utopia" means "no place." I could hear his mind rattling like coins in a jelly jar.

We all heard it.

A goldfish offered its version of the room. A little boy enacted splendid battles on the rug. Just you, me, and the machinery, baby.

Hold the light steady. Right, but it could fall apart as soon as I let go.

After I apologize for practically everything.

The silence collaborative... Kittenish in clover... She calculated the circumference and wrote the number on my forehead.

I strained to grasp the distinction between being found and getting found. Well, who made you president?

In the end we were sleeping with beepers.

Thus she concluded that beauty was real but was always accidental. He could have averted his eyes but he didn't. Something had torn a hole in the screen.

Which there are too many damn books in the house. Voicemail as weapon of choice.

The spider changed his mind and went the other way.

Blue jay / lawnmower. Blue jay / blue jay / blue jay. I contributed financially to their efforts to escape history.

She placed a stray feather in the dish as a counterweight. The dust supported multiple gravities.

Some were beaten, some were shot execution-style.

We stopped to breathe. Luckily there was no dearth of theory. She acquired those child-raising skills during her days as a calf roper.

What it came down to, he admitted, is too many young men and not enough mastodons. Well, well, well.

Suddenly a knock on the door: two evangelists for interspecies play.

I know that I know that. But we can't figure out why he won't intervene. Like when you were four and you fell into the septic tank.

Assertion / erasure. And peerless the raven breastplate of the flicker.

Truth is another matter.

× × ×

Ducks on the pond, crows in the road. Emphasis: the habit of using
the infinite as a standard usually results in irony. See, I got that from
Plotinus.

Pillow / plate / spoon. There was always the option of reversed worlds.

But whenever the swami said "Detach," she thought about violets.

They couldn't decide whether to enter the morning regatta or the
evening regatta. Herons hunting fingerlings. Wonder Woman counted
the babies and declared her work was done.

The landlord found him unconscious in the shower in an alcoholic
blackout. When I got an opportunity to complain I took it.

In the next installment the trained assassin sees the error of his ways.

Determined to get home before dark, the ant carried a dead lacewing
down the sidewalk. The minnows in the fish trap expired slowly as the
tide ran out. Honey, first the pants then the shoes.

He milked the law of unintended consequences for all it was worth. The
kids were learning, but they had to kill a lot of things in the process.

Okay now I'll be the mudflat and you be the barn swallow.

The now / the not yet. The wallet-sized snapshot. What do you mean I'm
not happy?

When it was over, her boyfriend figured a spaghetti dinner would be
good. That year they sliced one day out of each week and mailed it to the
future.

She worked the nightshift taking dictation from bats.

XXX

Halfway into the crossing, the man flung his Rolodex into the sea. Were they pelagic gulls or escaped balloons? That is one busy bee.

Nope it was a zebra longwing. But you have a choice.

He began, "My obligation to explain this to you does not imply that I find it excusable."

They hacked the spacetime continuum and put a shortcut to Valhalla on my desktop. She became a mathematician in the womb after hearing the word *parabola* spoken by a railman. He gave her the water, but it wasn't the water she was expecting.

The grab bag contained six sleepless nights. Whereas in our culture there are at least fifty-one synonyms for desire.

An entire generation defied the statistics but only once.

Free lunar eclipse! They hung a sign on the gate to warn the neighbors: beware of dictionary. Yo dude to fry some eggs you have to spill some milk.

Please be us, pretty please. We pieced together the icons our grandparents had smashed and thus arose a market for collectibles.

Stones, stones, stones—and these weren't from any kidney I knew.

He torched his to-do list and planted anemones. You can keep on looking if you insist. It was always the here and now versus the there and then.

We're circling the subject yes because the subject is circular. Last week was amphibious.

Vernal pools, just to say it.

Toast / fried onions. Cairns marked the trail above treeline. Goldenrod and shepherd's purse were singled out for euthanasia.

The whale was such a ruined motif, she used the striped bass instead. Definition of a priori: no jello without a mold.

So I'll wait.

Recent artifacts suggest that the art of accounting predates the art of love. The philosopher petted his cat and felt better. Through prior arrangement he received all communiqués from the spirit world through the daily chess notes.

Will you look at that madcap virus. It's as if everyone is colorblind and your job is to invent the rainbow.

Things escalate when he slaps a restraining order on my shoofly pie.

She hit the nail on the head and the nail was not surprised. You ain't the only exile on this block, Rocko. How much rope were you needing?

The bank teller knew the answer but kept silent. An oak leaf.

The edge of.

Still, a smart sparrow may occasionally outwit a dumb hawk. This was her genius, to be a confection in an age of masquerade and a masquerade in an age of confection. Roses / thorns.

An overwhelming majority of order Lepidoptera adopted Hegel's dialectic as a credo. Goosedown before the wind.

We were foxed by a number of invisible events.

Disneyland? Disney World? Remind me again which one this is? We have by no means seen the end of the doctrine of automatic harmony. Thus another pogrom provoked by translation error.

No, I felt like a stranger because I was a stranger. The salt of metaphysical sweat.

And so it was war: man versus molehill.

Shall we get this meeting started? A gray squirrel addressed us in no uncertain terms. His report concluded that light still works the way it always has.

They argued for hours about the state flower. Because *sturm und drang* does sell newspapers.

We could just tape it together for now.

The barmaid kept beaming me telegrams. Today's votive: acorn cap with cypress spurge. She stepped quickly across, then turned and waited on the other side.

We danced a little, then discussed the biomass till closing. The fundamentals of punctuation made a last pathetic stand.

Creaturehood struck him thunderously from behind.

A sensurround of arabesques. The artichokes would not recant. Their holiday bonfire underwent a leap of faith in the direction of the neighbor's gazebo.

At once the vanguard were drunken windbags and the remnant was clueless. More molecules than usual drifted north.

I felt acutely our separation from the fishes.

From a Catalogue for a Colorist

I take an oak leaf by the window of a dreamer
      I take disturbed cirrus
I take an empty crossroads and a false stair
I take what draws forward
I take a box lit from within
      I take a wheel out of round out of out out of round
I take what is concentric but not mendable

I take a lost ant, bearer of fictions

I take the frost because it is free
      I take the paisley verge of meadows
I take roll out and plug in
I take a crash of hexagonal magnitude
I take a clothespin on my fingertip
      I take oxhide
I take pitch

I take dried blood

I take sparrow breast
      I take a squash blossom and save it for a torch
I take a boy spinning bar stools
I take wisteria in velvet and a quiver of Chinese iris
I take an obscured coastline
      I take a coffin of ice
I take adamantine

I take one countersunk nail

I take a flock of faces downtown
        I take a pine knot right out of the paneling
I take an echo of our original cavern
I take what started what
I take lunch pail and back of the book
        I take snakeskin
I take car alarm

I take suggestions for my place of rest

I take inside a cup
        I take afterwards
I take a glass ball swirling atmospherics
I take its frozen lapidary feathers
I take memory of thirst
        I take tongues and belief
I take a spear tip for impaling worlds

I take paper peeled from paper

I take a floating canopy
        I take what it isn't
I take the day we had to knock down the wasps
I take it burnt to half-articulate
I take disappearing frames
        I take slants and stampings
I take an invading veil of shadow

I take what happened there next

I take those mad propellermen beetles
        I take the speckled bark of a beech tree in my friend's backyard

I take the words "edge of blacktop" and spray paint them on the edge of
    the blacktop
I take a developmental reversal with stupid hope
I take egg yolk
        I take berries
I take the center of the flame and its unerasable afterimage

I take the canvas above our heads

I take a stone bench where sit children inspecting a map
        I take thunder near and distant
I take a toy windup ambulance
I take the top left corner of the room and replace it with something similar
I take high tide
        I take reef knots and a random paramecium
I take the shoes of the innocent

I take the innocent

⚹ ⚹ ⚹

Let water be pour down
Let bone be whole
Let string be slip knot
Let fire be carry

Let breath be sing out
Let mist be cleft
Let seed be every
Let blood be thunder

⚹ ⚹ ⚹

With women sitting cross-legged in rowboats
        With knapweed and a grief-struck squirrel
With columns of rain to southeast
I take a clove hitch fastened to a fence rail

With late-season fireworks and my folding chair
　　　　With a heavy downpour at first light
With wrong-sized wire nuts and a lot of ocelots
I take the mariposa lily tattooed on your wrist

I take names at the honor killing
　　　　I take a photo of all of us there
With what could have been and might have occurred
I take that firmly in mind

With a potato for safety's sake
　　　　I take my uniform off at home
With feedback only at gunpoint
I take that lily pad you were standing on

With starfish from a snorkler
　　　　I take a formula for blessedness
With white herons and a snowy egret
I take a vow of silence and break it now

I take a reflux of doublethink and leave the drumming to others
　　　　I take compound umbels from wild carrot with permission
With nine kinds of wet grass
I take this briny ooze

With dusk on Thursday
　　　　With a file from the drawer
With calipers from the indigent caliperless
I take crossed fishlines, and then I take the bait

With a panful of cutlets standing in marinade
　　　　With the last slot in the parking garage
With the one who comes who is unknown
I take in stride your triple quadrupole mass spectrometer

With training in musical whistling
        I take a ticket to the May-hunt
With an auspicious December moth
I take a crescent moon caught in brambles and belabor it

With voicemail from radiolarians
        I take asparagus worldwide today
With a yogi from the empyrean
I take your bit part in the harlequinade

I take a diplodocus by alpenglow and a table of cubic measure
        I take cost-push and demand-pull to rash extremes
With a fat cat and a grass widow and an ingénue
I take a base on balls

With the law of independent assortment and the universe of discourse
        With a heterodox hatband and an x-intercept to Tasmania
With martyrologists and rally-masters
I take your meaning and wipe the phosphenes from my eyelids

With your wherewithal in addition to your whereabouts
        With the remainder as nontrivial
With earthshine and grapevines
I take maladroit from the quahog and call it okay

I take an uncool crosscut with brio
        I take a turn for the worse after the comet departs
With a quick nip, I mean nap
I take a jumping bean down my knickers

With a degree day and a thirty-second avalanche
        I take ostentation to the poop deck
With equestrians and aerialists and lacunae and schemata
I take a number and a letter to the sandlot

With contumely and pneumatics and autographs from herbalists
      I take a raincoat off a contralto with contrition
With an immersible verbal at octillion deeps
I take a lynx at his word

          ✕ ✕ ✕

Let water
Let bone
Let string
Let fire

Be pour down
Be whole
Be slip knot
Be carry

          ✕ ✕ ✕

I record the invention of the howitzer and the capri pant, though not in
    this century
      O I wait there for wilderness to call
I prefer what's left once you punch cookies out
I swear to house rules
I make a play for the starry crown and a song they put it in
      I discharge a thousand faxes from yesterday
I relinquish my turtle specimens at last
I calculate as equivalent to five clumps of violets
I graduate to pointing, not speaking
      I establish protocol for used jars
I select hypnotic immersion and give a wrench to my pillow
I think about darning bald spots in the lawn
I change hands
      I save myself for biofuel
I struggle with servant mind and assertion of the nonself

I seep toward evening with an inky look

I join the great transposon mutiny
        I refer a photograph of a pie to the pie itself
I pull Anthony dollars from my ears
I cause an inadvertent ruckus
I massage the magus and deliver his correlations
        I multiply by a quotient of his first incisor
I cultivate pencil points
I print clearly my name on a cellophane pane of the wing of a dragonfly
I assign ten to left and ten to right
        I lay my hands on you later
I circle the wrong bottle cap
I await a wilder lettuce
I jerk all four seasons, to postliterate applause
        I chafe at Do Not Enter
I lose track of cecropia moths for nearly a minute

I set this map at full scale

I mean everything and understand nothing
        I eat my spare silk
I testify to the revolt of my sleeves
I sprinkle extra space
I go steady with a prehistorian
        I unearth a humerus bone from humus
I determine mine to be the only body in that well
I stack newspapers six ways from Sunday
I pack the undercroft and preach to the overhead
        I persuade it to join my board of directors
I return from the dead, this time with a sandwich
I crack dumb jokes about dust
I bear a minnow's standard among the colonnades
        I observe ember day in my own special way
I propose duplicate bridge as a model for political economy

I surrender a moist towelette

I boil salt soup for the prophets
     I medal in a dark sport
I quarterfold distance and outrun lava
I wend landward with my variocoupler
I accuse the clerk of choplogic
     I sort my collection of inflorescence
I bend a shape to hold down the hillside
I count that one against you
I fiddle up the vermiform
     I introduce the xenolith to the regolith
I annotate zinnia
I peddle koans to a dolmen
I bind your tongue to the last breath of a stranger
     I rip out the recipe for serendipity trout
I raise discalced to a new level

I yawn in the face of a pastedown

⨯ ⨯ ⨯

Let water be thunder
Let bone be cleft
Let string be carry
Let fire be every

Let breath be slip knot
Let mist be whole
Let seed be sing out
Let blood be pour down

⨯ ⨯ ⨯

If you ever If you never If you advisedly If you humanly
If you arrestingly If you afterwards If you doubly If you not at all

If you creepily If you crawlingly If you mightily If you spitefully
If you pointedly If you winterly If you flagrantly If you underneath

If you patiently If you obliquely If you ploddingly If you plinkingly
If you beeperly If you beingly If you invectively If you actually

If you possibly If you finally If you dearly If you darkly
If you barely If you blindly If you belatedly If you beratingly

If you ribbonly If you robinly If you rashly If you radishly
If you evenly If you oceanly If you leafingly If you laughingly

If you singly If you multiply If you in situ If you wherever
If you on one hand If you on the other If you now If you later

If you soberly If you stupidly If you coldly If you very
If you bristly If you beggarly If you meadowly If you maybe

If you rhetorically If you cholerically If you vastly If you placidly
If you above If you below If you hardly If you not yet

✕ ✕ ✕

Let breath
Let mist
Let seed
Let blood

Be sing out
Be cleft
Be every
Be thunder

✕ ✕ ✕

Rock turns into stone, then back into rock
Man bites another man, but only on pinky
        Sand develops alternatives
Thistle stands in for it

Doubt calls up a swan, then a swan boat
       Certainty tolls the hour

Insomniac earwigs swarm gladiolas
Druids invade
       Water oak scared of own shadow
Screech owl recites credo: hallelujah

Priestess reveals final prime number
       Universe would rather not

Accident reconstructionist claims to analyze culture clash
Meadow remains unchurched
       Night arrives before ferry
Neighbor gets clarinet

Girls trail swallowtails across avenue
       Traffic vanishes through magic porthole

Artist likes paintings best sideways
Tunisian hall and stair disprove laws of perspective
       Boy holding can punks boy holding candle
Ice water sometimes good for veins

More fits into envelope than previously thought
       Blowfish wishes to be left alone

Water table voids covenant with dowser
Palmers appear in great numbers along arborway
       Man kidnaps ex-girlfriend's crocodile
Plastic container snaps shut

Grocer accepts geometry proofs in exchange
       Incendiary bombs not just for weekend use

Diaphanous tires of the rigmarole
Fruit bat quits mammals
    Tinfoil brain crinkles
Clerk swears eyeballs in pocket are his

Bitter stream washes gravestones of fathers
    Children expected to feel excision

Majorettes referee refugees
Promise stands a lower molar's chance
    Grassblades first to notice
Cross in question is Maltese

Dry nurse dry-mops dry ice
    No close relative found for butter or commonsense

Bank opens lichen repository
Jellyfish not a sign of end times
    Mail carrier admits to extra trips around rotary
Basilisk tears cure that, insists homeopathist

President guarantees mattress discounts
    Orb weaver named to cabinet

Actual things not the same as ideas about things
Woman signals from rear pew
    Stratosphere sues ionosphere
Tide waits for once

Imaginary apples key to famine relief
    Cruet found in back of cupboard

Whelk applies for witness protection
Purple rebrands as violet
    Reindeer strike for more moss, fewer mosquitoes
Lack of scrap bewilders quilters in three counties

Open sentence snags on sweaters
  That snapshot not the best one of you lately

Hod carrier admits to novice status
Hirelings frost icehouse for fun
  Local man called
Angel pens tell-all

⨯ ⨯ ⨯

> *Let water be carry*
> *Let bone be sing out*
> *Let string be thunder*
> *Let fire be pour down*
>
> *Let breath be every*
> *Let mist be whole*
> *Let seed be slip knot*
> *Let blood be cleft*

⨯ ⨯ ⨯

She studies cave crickets
  They say, *all praise the myth of the fig marigold*
She studies wood shavings
  They say, *compare me to a summer's day*
She studies broken lampstands and trail cairns above treeline
  They say, *remember fidelity*
She studies paperclips
  They say, *I do*

She studies the powers coming in and going out
  They say, *there's a spider on your collar*
She studies a fallen aspen and a disemboweled field mouse
  They say, *give a dollar to that homeless man on the median strip*
She studies beatniks and gangsters
  They say, *drape us in moss pink*

She studies instant replays
They say, *the Buddha was right*

She studies mute swans
They say, *we would kill you if we could*
She studies quetzals
They say, *new motifs for motorbikes*
She studies economic theory and the aquatic schooling instinct
They say, *call the kingfisher down from his perch*
She studies her errors
They say distinctly, *quince*

She studies leopards and leopard frogs
They say, *not in this life*
She studies irregular polygons
They say, *narcoleptic spectacles draped in moonlight*
She studies gates and dolmens
They say, *pin your geopolitics to the Mercator projection*
She studies bituminous coal and diatomaceous earth
They say, *tell him yourself*

She studies how the draglines attach
They say, *sahib, here comes the haboob*
She studies woodchucks eating windfall apples
They say, *we seek not the face of God*
She studies yttrium and ytterbium
They say, *we can hear the dust land*
She studies water striders
They say, *seraphs in sequins*

She studies her dew-soaked shoes
They say, *rose path at a distance*
She studies the mind and the brain
They say, *incinerate whatever you can*
She studies the gills of a panther cap mushroom
They say, *lamellae*

She studies the multitudinum and the vitreous humor
>They say, *thank you, bivalves, for all that siphoning*

She studies fifth wheels and third parties
>They say, *v-notch in the tail of a swallow*

She studies the 39 parts of a cow
>They say, *frosted, fluted, dimpled, drizzled, speckled, sparkled, crumpled, crackled*

She studies everyone's intentions
>They say, *unyielding ache at periphery*

She studies diphthongs
>They say, *cumulonimbus*

She studies incidental tales of neverending rearending
>They say, *pace off your sample space*

She studies incarnations
>They say, *just as you suspected*

She studies totemic animals stamped on coins
>They say, *address your sombrero*

She studies bats over train tracks
>They say, *implements left by the dead*

Ꭓ Ꭓ Ꭓ

Let water
Let bone
Let string
Let fire

Be thunder
Be cleft
Be carry
Be every

Ꭓ Ꭓ Ꭓ

He carries bergamot in his packsaddle
       He carries a book over his heart
He seeks a path through ocotillo
He knows: the field is the world

He watches matter congeal around a singularity
       He watches traffic stack up in a sideview mirror
He seeks himself during intermission
He knows: alabaster for impediments

He destroys his last conversation by fire in a pine hollow
       He destroys fence posts when he sleepwalks
He seeks the submerged village of his soul
He knows: it could be a jest

He invents a dormitory for his weekend thoughts
       He invents an algebraist around the corner
He seeks a camshaft to soothe his tempers
He knows: a lark evermore

He carries larks in his packsaddle
       He carries a camshaft in his heart
He seeks a solution for x that will stick
He knows: these lodging are temporary

He watches his soul congeal around a simplicity
       He watches for dragging hooks
He seeks boundaries for infinitude
He knows: dry pine for kindling

He destroys his last intermission by fire
       He destroys impediments when he sleepwalks
He seeks history mapped to a grid
He knows: messages tend to an outskirts

He invents worlds over the weekend
     He invents ocotillo to feel better
He seeks words for that banging in his temple
He knows: *bergamot* may be among them

He carries larks and bergamot in his packsaddle
     He carries a camshaft banging in his heart
He seeks ocotillo as a solution
He knows: material awaits a maker

He watches from the outskirts of simplicity
     He watches history dredge the lake
He seeks a gate to walk through, as foretold
He knows: fire stops nothing

He destroys his last pine barren during intermission
     He destroys fox tracks with fresh snowfall
He seeks evidence on the fishhook
He knows: his soul is on exhale

He invents a flat place and stands there
     He invents numeracy while debating with sand
He seeks engagement with tidal sources
He knows: a backpack is ringing

He carries larks singing in his chest
     He carries a tide turning pages
He seeks a variable for sand in the algebraist's syntax
He knows: from there he could see the next landscape

He watches the shape his soul condenses in cold air
     He watches fish rise to their mirror
He seeks fox tracks in mud at stone walls
He knows: he won't cross over

He destroys stoplights erected on the mountain
     He destroys his alabaster idols
He seeks a lake that will tell him something
He knows: to expect manifold centers

He invents the first seed, after reading the footnotes
     He invents an equation for smoke
He seeks a language for circular motion
He knows: he carries bergamot in his packsaddle.

✕ ✕ ✕

Let water be sing out
Let bone be slip knot
Let string be every
Let fire be cleft

Let breath be thunder
Let mist be pour down
Let seed be whole
Let blood be carry

✕ ✕ ✕

Is your hand on my arm just now
Is opening a soul window at the moment of death
Is older and wiser than a sand dollar
Is the chief end of love
Is what you know when you know it
Is hoping the furnace will kick in
Is wrapping a sandwich for the road
     Is the canoe of fate on a postcard

Is prying boards off the barn
Is heavier than if you carried it yourself
Is not getting better anytime soon
Is merely a suggestion
Is why you remind me of porcupines

Is everything you wanted to say but was not allowed to
Is an obstacle course for the foolhardy
        Is a forest of peonies

Is looking away from that wreckage
Is only found in Samoa
Is singing with children after a potluck
Is help you never dreamed you would need
Is a swingset in snow
Is gibbous if you say so
Is always in your eyes, though you deny it
        Is leaning on a locked gate

Is a mildly fortuitous fender bender
Is going to find the ferryman
Is scratched on your heart as you enter this world
Is a question you could ask
Is a stripe you have painted between us
Is wavier than anyone remembers
Is unobtrusive in this photo
        Is planning to rise up through the asphalt

Is dancing a fandango in a dark courtyard
Is slipping a cipher into your pocket
Is a blue heron stalking shallows
Is a message you missed with the tide
Is abiding, as ever
Is the aroma of burnt cornsilk
Is a man tapping a microphone
        Is a sentinel propped on an outcropping

Is proof you said you were seeking
Is battered by sunshine before you arrive
Is somersaulting among the alfalfa
Is often served with raspberry
Is punctuated for survival

Is shackled to wonder and sentenced to wander
Is mingling expertly in the canteen
    Is proposing to silence on a banished keyboard

Is raining acorns all morning
Is measuring you the old-fashioned way
Is worse than salad at midnight
Is a ring toss in the deep end
Is wood coals fizzing in a metal bucket
Is sorcery under a pen name
Is feeling a raven fly through
    Is as mercy among the nannoplankton

Is disguised as a beast epic to avoid detection
Is only wax resist for beginners
Is welding while distracted
Is cotangent at present
Is setting a bed for you on the roof tonight
Is flashing your name from shipboard
Is written in squid ink
    Is light leaking from somewhere

⚥ ⚥ ⚥

Let breath
Let mist
Let seed
Let blood

Be slip knot
Be whole
Be sing out
Be pour down

⚥ ⚥ ⚥

So I put down my pistol and pick up my pickaxe
      I sluice three gutters of west wind
I arabesque at laundromats
I drop a popcorn trail across your digression
I trap a paper wasp in a paper cup
      I throw a party in my carport
I pledge my innards and translate fire to the high steppes
I meet in mufti with monarchs
I astral-project into schooling bluefish without an agenda
      I chop roses from concertina wire
I reach for my Allen wrench
I heft coral and grope for its knucklebone
I seduce a drawstring and wring elegies from floor mops
      I monitor hearts of palm
I sign to my oven for more sweet potatoes

I register early for a boat-shaped grave

I haunt dry corners
      I sleep under lacebark pine
I patrol rooflines for oriole assassins
I pile Precambrian discs where rockhounds will find them
I defuse a steak bomb
      I take it apart and reassemble it later in an unlikely location
I switch on my mirror neurons
I rip up your payday loan on the eighth day
I unpack my avian epaulets
      I secret Clovis points into my shirt
I wise up on orthotics
I make the mahout move over
I mourn with all herbivores their lost forests
      I hold harmless only the honeybees
I apply a positive valance to a negative pole

I suffer a parallax

I inherit the Great Red Spot and copyright further reference
      I choose between boas and pythons
I salute a golden larch
I slide a tile toward you
I gaze past to the landscape beyond
      I believe I hear bluebells
I disciple a plumb line
I intend overcapacity
I tailgate fireflies
      I shout when the shouting is over
I proceed as if the unit block is indivisible
I suspect the snow monkeys of intercession
I chuckle over the intercom
      I turn to gyrfalcons for a response
I figure-skate past conflagrations

I come unglued in the bath

I caucus with lentils and bow out of the foofaraw
      I privilege magenta
I umlaut sparingly
I desire to smack the deanery
I hesitate before the iron-hearted
      I converse with this regarding that
I confuse moonlight with marmalade
I thresh and grow mighty
I sew saffron robes for a sadsack sailor
      I decline the incline
I greet a polynomial with joy
I array food and drink before it
I question the authority granted to scrimshaw
      I construct a new wing when things feel crowded
I recognize these ingredients from somewhere

I cancel the damned redaction

Notes

In "Parts List Counted in Ogham" italicized quotes, in order of appearance, are borrowed from Paul Tillich, Martin Buber, Joseph Campbell, Wendell Berry, William James, Thomas Merton, John Milton, Jane Lead, Virginia Woolf, Dietrich Bonhoeffer, Denise Levertov, Lucretius, Mary Daly, G. K. Chesterton, Flannery O'Connor, Julian of Norwich, Anonymous, Rainer Maria Rilke, Søren Kierkegaard, and Margaret Sanger.

The lyrics at the end of "Questions of Scale" are from an old Irish folksong. An exact meaning for "the dear knows" is a matter for argument. Some traditions suggest it may be a safe way to say "the devil knows" so as not to summon him in the event that he is listening.

"All is linked" in "Extracurricular" is drawn from this passage from Liebniz: "In every possible world, everything is linked together (tout est lié). The universe—however it might be constituted—is a unified whole, like an ocean; even the smallest motion extends its influence to any distance, however large." From Nicholas Rescher, *On Liebniz: Expanded Edition*.

"Testimony Concerning Diatoms" includes a fragment from these lines of Philip Whalen in "Sourdough Mountain Lookout": "Then I'm alone in a glass house on a ridge/Encircled by chiming mountains/With one sun roaring through the house all day/& the others crashing through the glass all night/Conscious even while sleeping." The fragment "A ghost dancer walks . . ." is from Thomas Merton, *The Geography of Lograire*.

"Lost Gospel of Ribosome" germinated in this passage from Matt Ridley's book *Genome:* "Before the discovery of the genome, we did not know there was a document at the heart of every cell three billion letters long of whose content we knew nothing."

"From a Catalogue for a Colorist" is a partial translation of Gerhard Richter's painting *4096 Colors*.

Acknowledgments

Many thanks to the editors of the following publications, where earlier versions of these poems first appeared:

Blackbird: "From a Catalogue for a Colorist"

Conjunctions: "Parts List Counted in Ogham"

Mudlark: "Nine Pictographs and a Slight Correlation to a Lyric by Elvis"

Thanks also to Dr. Tatiana Rynearson at the University of Rhode Island Graduate School of Oceanography, who welcomed me into her plankton lab for an afternoon. I am grateful for the enthusiasm and example of kind friends and poets, especially Maya Smith Janson and Sharon White, and for biochemistry conversation with Marcie Glicksman, who so gets why I love ribosomes.

I thank David Baggarly for generous permission to use his beautiful painting *Aut Icon, #9* as a cover image.

This book is for Walker Rumble, always my first reader, my companion, *mi cielo.*

About the Lexi Rudnitsky Editor's Choice Award

The Lexi Rudnitsky Editor's Choice Award is given annually to a poetry collection by a writer who has published at least one previous book of poems. Along with the Lexi Rudnitsky First Book Prize in Poetry, it is a collaboration of Persea Books and the Lexi Rudnitsky Poetry Project. Entry guidelines for both awards are available on Persea's website (www.perseabooks.com).

Lexi Rudnitsky (1972–2005) grew up outside of Boston, and studied at Brown University and Columbia University. Her own poems exhibit both a playful love of language and a fierce conscience. Her writing appeared in *The Antioch Review, Columbia: A Journal of Literature and Art, The Nation, The New Yorker, The Paris Review, Pequod,* and *The Western Humanities Review.* In 2004, she won the Milton Kessler Memorial Prize for Poetry from *Harpur Palate.*

Lexi died suddenly in 2005, just months after the birth of her first child and the acceptance for publication of her first book of poems, *A Doorless Knocking into Night* (Mid-List Press, 2006). The Lexi Rudnitsky book prizes were created to memorialize her by promoting the type of poet and poetry in which she so spiritedly believed.

PREVIOUS WINNERS OF THE LEXI RUDNITSKY EDITOR'S CHOICE AWARD:

2014	Shane McCrae	*The Animal Too Big to Kill*
2013	Caki Wilkinson	*The Wynona Stone Poems*
2012	Michael White	*Vermeer in Hell*
2011	Mitchell L. H. Douglas	*blak al-febet*
2010	Amy Newman	*Dear Editor*